IMAGES
of America

MAINE'S TWO-FOOTER
RAILROADS
THE LINWOOD MOODY
COLLECTION

Linwood Moody took this self portrait in the early 1930s. Selfies are not just a recent phenomenon. (Courtesy of the Linwood Moody Collection.)

IMAGES
of America

MAINE'S TWO-FOOTER RAILROADS
THE LINWOOD MOODY COLLECTION

Michael W. Torreson

ARCADIA
PUBLISHING

Copyright © 2024 by Michael W. Torreson
ISBN 978-1-4671-0937-6

Published by Arcadia Publishing
Charleston, South Carolina

Printed in the United States of America

Library of Congress Control Number: 2023947588

For all general information, please contact Arcadia Publishing:
Telephone 843-853-2070
Fax 843-853-0044
E-mail sales@arcadiapublishing.com

Visit us on the Internet at www.arcadiapublishing.com

To Linwood Moody, a man of many skills—a pioneer railroad photographer, prolific letter writer who corresponded with over 200 pen pals on a monthly basis for much of his adult life, small-town depot agent, magazine publisher, author, and dry humorist.

CONTENTS

ACKNOWLEDGMENTS

First off, thanks to Linwood Moody for writing his book *The Maine Two-Footers*, which was my first railroad book, purchased in 1968 from the Colorado Railroad Museum.

Also prominently, I would like to thank Laura Winter of Estherville Printing for all her help with computer skills, which included photograph scanning and much more.

Big thanks go to the family of the late Robert C. Jones, author of the two-volume book *Two Feet Between The Rails*. Jim Jones was very helpful in giving his encouragement and blessing for this book.

Thanks to Arcadia Publishing's Caroline (Anderson) Vickerson for her help and encouragement in getting this book finished, providing a couple deadline extensions along the way.

Thanks go to Dr. Russell Martin of the DeGolyer Foundation of Dallas, Texas, where most of Linwood's railroad negatives and photographs reside and are available to interested parties.

I must also thank my two house cats Smokey and Chester (Chetter), who have taken a keen interest in the preparation of this book.

Lastly and very importantly, I would like to thank all the members of the museums that have brought back to life some of the Maine two-foot railroads: the Wiscasset, Waterville & Farmington Railway Museum at Alna, Maine; the Sandy River & Rangeley Lakes Railroad at Phillips, Maine; and the Maine Narrow Gauge Railroad and Museum of Portland, Maine. All the members have contributed a huge amount of time, money, and hard work to enable us to experience a real operating Maine two-foot narrow-gauge railroad.

Unless otherwise noted, all images appear courtesy of the Linwood Moody Collection.

INTRODUCTION

As the cover of this book mentions, Linwood W. Moody (July 17, 1905–July 13, 1983) retained a box of around 500 sentimental photographs that he personally took of three of Maine's two-foot-gauge railroads. The Wiscasset, Waterville & Farmington Railway (WW&F); the Sandy River & Rangeley Lakes Railroad (SR&RL, also referred to as the Sandy River); and the Monson Railroad. Moody retained this box of photographs until his death in 1983.

I suspect he may have had another box of photographs with the other Maine two-footer railroads—the Bridgton & Saco River Railroad/Bridgton & Harrison Railroad, the Kennebec Central Railroad, and the Edaville Railroad—but that box is lost to history.

The good news is that the DeGolyer Foundation of Dallas, Texas, has most of Moody's negatives, so these other three two footers are represented there and are available to anyone interested. Most of these photographs have been published in numerous books over the years.

The most interesting aspect of these photographs is Moody's notes on the back of each image providing details and dates that he took the photograph and even the time in several instances. In these notes, one can create a timeline of his trips to photograph three of the two-foot-gauge railroads covered in this book.

A mini roster of the locomotives is as follows: The SR&RL/Sandy River had 10 locomotives in 1932. Three were 0-4-4 Forney type No. 17 (operational) and No. 21 and No. 22 (stored). Two 2-4-4 Forney types, No. 9 and No. 10, were both operational, and of the five 2-6-2 tender engines, No. 16, No. 18, No. 19, No. 23, and No. 24, only No. 18 and No. 24 were operational after the summer of 1933. No. 16 was in operation until the fall of 1933, when her boiler tubes expired. She joined No. 19 and No. 23 in storage in the 10-stall roundhouse in Phillips, Maine.

As of 1933, the WW&F had five 0-4-4 Forney type locomotives, No. 2, No. 3, No. 4, No. 8, and No. 9. In addition, the WW&F had one 2-4-4 Forney, No. 7, and one 2-6-2 tender engine, No. 6. All but the No. 8 and No. 9 were out of service by 1933.

The Monson Railroad had but two locomotives, No. 3 and No. 4, both 0-4-0 Forneys. They were in operation until the Monson Railroad ceased operation in 1943.

Linwood Moody's book *The Maine Two-Footers* was Howell North Book's bestseller. He was getting royalty checks from it almost until the time of his death in 1983.

Moody worked for railroads all his adult life until his retirement, beginning with the Georges Valley Railroad/Knox Railroad and ending with the Belfast & Mooshead Lake Railroad as a depot agent at Brooks, Maine. He actually worked one day at the WW&F Railway in 1932 but quit after finding out owner Frank Winter had not given him an accurate job description. He was hired as superintendent, but when he arrived for work, he found out he was to be the station agent at Albion during the day and engine watchman during the night, all for $18 per week.

Moody also worked for Ellis Atwood helping to locate locomotives and equipment for the Edaville Railroad at South Carver, Massachusetts, from 1945 to 1947. Most of the extant Maine two-foot-gauge rolling stock was located and ended up at Atwood's Edaville Railroad by 1947, with the exception of WW&F Railway No. 9, which had previously been Kennebec Central Railroad No. 4, and SR&RL Railroad No. 6. It survives in operation in 2023 at the Wiscasset, Waterville & Farmington Railway Museum at Sheepscot Station, just a few miles north of Wiscasset, Maine.

Online, one can find more about Linwood Moody at kalloch.org, where a nice obituary of him was written by Ellis Spear of Warren, Maine, titled "Hidden under Bushels." I would encourage the reader to check it out.

Moody also operated a photographic service for many years from the 1930s until he sold his negative collection in 1959 to the DeGolyer Foundation. His letterhead listed the following services: photo finishing, commercial photography, camera supplies, job printing, etchings and engravings, and printer supplies. At the top he listed "Publishers of Moody's Magazine" with his name in capital letters and "General Photography & Printing" below in red letters, followed by his address of P.O. Box 144, Union, Maine. He also was editor of the Belfast & Moosehead Lake Railroad employee magazine the *Waycar*, and editor of the *Bogger* for Ellis Atwood's Edaville Railroad.

One interesting story about my experience as a pen pal of Moody's was the opportunity to join him for his birthday on July 17, 1982. As it turned out, this birthday was his last, as he passed away the next year just a few days shy of turning 78.

The challenge was that Moody would only communicate by letter. This meant that I had to travel half a continent with no way of knowing for sure if it would all work as planned. It did work out great in the end. At the appointed time, we arrived at Phillips, Maine, accompanied by my longtime friend Rich Wilkinson in his fuel efficient Volkswagen Rabbit Diesel. At 11:00 a.m. at the Phillips Depot of the SR&RL, Moody and his old friend Homan (who worked with Moody at his hometown railroad in the late 1920s) showed up as promised and on time.

The first thing we all did was join Moody as he gave us a walking tour of the cemetery just behind the remains of the 10-stall roundhouse of the SR&RL. Many of the SR&RL employees are at their eternal rest just yards from where they spent years working for the Sandy River. Master mechanic Leland Stinchfield, conductor Bob McMullen, and many others were visited that day. Finally, we came to engineer Dana Aldrich's grave, where Linwood posed for a photograph by Aldrich's headstone. After that, we headed downtown and bought sandwiches and Pepsis for the planned picnic at Perham Junction right on Sluice Hill, the ruling grade of the SR&RL main line to Rangeley. Moody brought lawn chairs to sit in, and we all lunched in the shade right about where the switch to the Barnjum Branch was located. That leisurely lunch was followed by a return to the Phillips depot. I was fortunate to ride back in Moody's car, and he pointed out the sights as much of the railroad grade is now a gravel road. All too soon it was over, and Rich and I waved as Moody and Homan drove off on the grade of the SR&RL east of the depot and shop building in his Dodge Aspen (or aspirin, as he called it).

One

LINWOOD GETS ACQUAINTED WITH THE TWO FOOTERS IN 1932 AND 1933

Among Linwood Moody's notes, letters, and sentimental papers that were received from his coexecutor in 2006 was this scrap of note paper, which stands out from a historical perspective. Written in his handwriting, it lists his many trips to the largest of the Maine two footers, the Sandy River & Rangeley Lakes Railroad, headquartered in Phillips, Maine, from June 14, 1932, to the end of operations in July 1935. From this and notes on the back of his box of photographs, a timeline could be created of those railfan trips from the mid-1930s, which often included his friends Newell Martin, Peter Cornwall, and numerous others who shared his passion for the two footers. Often, they stood side by side as they photographed history for all to enjoy today.

To Phillips —

1. JUNE 14, 1932
2. JULY 27, 1933
3. MARCH 31, 1934
4. JUNE 20, 1934
5. JUNE 23, 1934
6. { JULY 17, 1934
    "   18
7. SEPT. 15 1934
           16
8. JAN. 18, 1935
9. APRIL 1, 1935
10. MAY 22, 1935
11. { JUNE 24, 1935
         25
         26
         27
12. { JULY 1, 1935
        2.
13. JULY 9, 1935
14. { JULY 13, 1935
        14.
15.

Before traveling up to Phillips for his first and only visit to the SR&RL in 1932, Moody stopped to visit the Wiscasset, Waterville & Farmington Railway (WW&F) at its base of operations at Wiscasset, Maine. This photograph shows the WW&F repair shops at Wiscasset. The date was May 22, 1932. Was this the time Moody asked owner Frank Winter for a job on the WW&F? Quite possibly.

While at the WW&F on May 22, 1932, Moody turned to snap this photograph of WW&F No. 6. It and No. 7 had been in the three-stall roundhouse that had burned the previous year. A marvelous re-creation of this roundhouse was opened in 2022 by the WW&F Railway Museum just north of Wiscasset at Sheepscot Station, Alna, Maine.

Here is another shot of WW&F No. 6 and No. 7 rusting away after the three-stall roundhouse burned while they were stored inside. They remained there until they were scrapped on-site several years later.

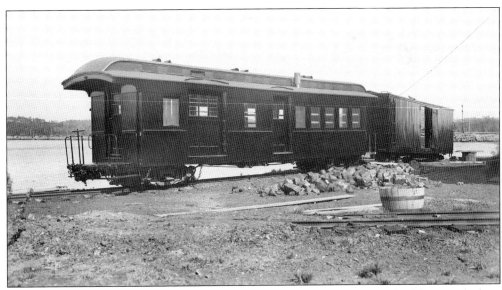

Behind the WW&F shop building on May 22, 1932, was Jackson & Sharpe–built baggage/railway post office/passenger car No. 6. Note the apparent recent paint job.

Also photographed on that day was baggage/RPO car No. 1. It was just a few yards north on the same siding as car No. 6.

On June 14, 1932, Moody parked on the other side of the Sandy River & Rangeley Lakes Railroad (SR&RL) depot/offices and snapped this view looking south between the depot and the fine brick shops/roundhouse complex. He had earlier stopped at Strong, Maine, where he witnessed not one but two Sandy River trains for the first time. He then drove on to Phillips for the first time.

Moody's notes on the back of this photograph indicate this caboose, No. 556, had just come in from Rangeley to tie up for the day. The train was an extra pulled by No. 24.

Walking from the depot where he snapped the previous photograph, Moody found No. 24 simmering in front of its stall at the end of the day after pulling the extra from Rangeley. June 14, 1932, was quite a lucky introduction to the largest of the two footers, the SR&RL. On this day, Moody witnessed three locomotives in steam, No. 10, No. 16, and No. 24.

A few steps later, Moody got a nice broadside shot of the beautiful No. 24. It was the newest of the SR&RL locomotives, built in 1919 by Baldwin Locomotive Works.

Here is SR&RL superintendent Orris Vose's stylish Model T railcar. On this day, Moody met Vose as well as many SR&RL employees for the first time.

The last photograph of Moody's first visit on June 14, 1932, was of REO railbus No. 5. The operator that day was engineer/fireman/railbus operator Ed West.

Later that month, on June 25, 1932, Moody was in Wiscasset at the WW&F Railway. This was the depot by the diamond crossing of the Maine Central Railroad's Rockland branch. It is likely that this is the day Moody arrived for work on the WW&F. In his book, he stated that he found that in addition to being hired by WW&F owner Frank Winter as "superintendent," he was also to be depot agent at Albion (the far north terminus of the WW&F) and nighttime engine watchman. He quit at the end of the day, apparently over the misrepresentation of the job description and the $18 per week salary. Moody later indicated that Winter was a rather intimidating man at six foot, four inches and was originally from the state of Iowa. Winter lived a very long life of 102 years.

WW&F Railway locomotive 0-4-4 No. 4 was built by Porter in 1901. This engine was in charge of the WW&F daily mixed train on June 25, 1932. Engineer Earl Keefe became a lifelong friend of Moody's; Linwood was a pallbearer at Keefe's funeral.

Forney type 0-4-4 No. 2 was in use on that day switching the lower yard at Wiscasset. At 18 tons, No. 2 and No. 3 were the only engines that could be used on the spindly trestle across the bay to the lower yard. In the background is the charred engine No. 6.

On June 15, 1933, the daily morning mixed train of the WW&F departed Albion at 5:30 a.m. and derailed between Whitefield and Head Tide at 7:33 a.m. This was the end of operations on the WW&F by rail. Frank Winter continued operations by truck for a short while after to carry the mail.

Moody, watch fob hanging from his right trouser pocket and a pipe in his mouth, poses the next day, June 16, 1933, with the poor, derailed WW&F No. 8. Later, it was scrapped on-site.

Not long after photographing the last train of the WW&F at its derailment site, Moody headed back to Phillips, Maine, to witness the reopened Sandy River & Rangeley Lakes Railroad. It had closed in July 1932 just after Moody's first visit. Here is an early morning shot of No. 24 heading up a mixed train and REO railbus No. 5 ready to head to Farmington on July 27, 1933.

The notes on the back of this photograph state this was the SR&RL roundhouse on July 27, 1933. From left to right, the engines are No. 22, No. 19 inside behind No. 22, No. 23 (in the second stall with door open), No. 9 (in the third stall), No. 18, No. 17, Orris Vose's Model T railcar No. 21, No. 10, No. 16 (in the ninth stall and under steam), and No. 24's stall. No. 24 had just left with the morning mixed train. This photograph was the first in a series Moody took at the request of master mechanic Leland Stinchfield. A thank-you letter from Stinchfield to Moody is in this book's last chapter.

No. 16 is about to pull No. 18 outside to be photographed. No. 16 was almost out of time on its boiler flues. This was one of the last times it was under steam before being stored, never to operate again.

No. 18 has been pulled outside to be photographed. No. 16 had uncoupled and backed on to the turntable for the photograph.

No. 10 came out next in its winter attire, as the locomotive was used mostly in the colder months in the final years of the SR&RL. The No. 10 is a Forney-type locomotive with an enclosed cab, which made it (and other Forney-type engines) quite attractive to use in the cold months due to the warmer working conditions.

After No. 10, No. 17 come out in the morning sun to be photographed. Also in winter attire, No. 17 often retained the mounted snowplow year-round as she and the other Forney-type locomotives (Nos. 9 and 10) were mostly used in winter operations.

Next, the largest of the Sandy River's locomotives, No. 23, came out for a portrait. It was never to operate again as its tubes had expired in 1931. Moody and some of his railfan friends later rode in the cab of No. 23 when it was moved to Strong prior to its scrapping in 1936.

On July 27, 1933, Supt. Orris Vose posed with his personal Model T railcar in front of the Phillips depot. This car has survived and can be seen today at the Maine Narrow Gauge Railroad and Museum in Portland.

Moody rode with Superintendent Vose over to Avon and Strong on July 27, 1933. Here, in Avon, the SR&RL's Model T railcar is being used by the section men out on the line.

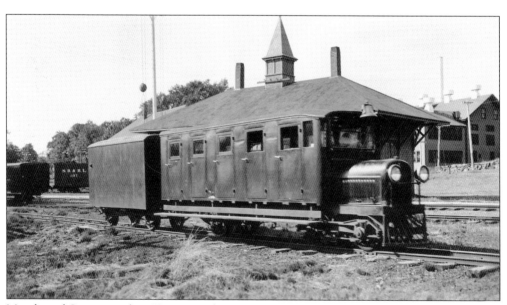

Moody and Superintendent Vose arrived at Strong just as SR&RL railbus No. 4 was coming in from Kingfield and Carrabasset. It would be turned on the turntable in front of the Strong depot. Right after that, Vose turned his Model T inspection car on the same turntable to return to Phillips. Moody had a very successful and memorable day indeed.

Two

SANDY RIVER OPERATIONS
IN 1933 AND 1934

In Moody's first trip to the SR&RL on March 31, 1934, he found No. 24 on the Strong turntable. On this day, longtime engineer Charles Hodgeman was in charge in the cab. Hodgeman had 56 years of service with the SR&RL and its predecessors.

Also in Strong on March 31, 1934, was 2-4-4 No. 10 with a short mixed train on its way back to Phillips. No. 10 was the second-youngest engine on the SR&RL, having been built by Baldwin Locomotive Works of Philadelphia, Pennsylvania, in 1916. Dana Aldrich was the engineer.

Back at Phillips later in the day, engineer Dana Aldrich oils the running gear on the engine. E'en Campbell fills the water tank before No. 10 is put away in the roundhouse.

SR&RL caboose No. 551 is parked at Phillips on that same sprint day, March 31. It was being looked over by one of Moody's railfan friends.

Out of service, No. 22 rested outside the last stall of the 10-stall roundhouse at Phillips. Moody's company that day, Newall Martin, poses as an SR&RL employee with oil can in hand. However, No. 22 would never move again, being scraped on this spot in July 1935 just after the final closure of the railroad. No. 22 was the first to be scrapped, followed by the entire railroad in 1935 and 1936.

Engineer/fireman Ed West (left) and Supt. Orris Vose pose by No. 9. It was in service until the end of operations of the SR&RL Railroad.

A few moments later, West and Vose stepped aside, and Moody snapped another photograph of No. 9. The locomotive was built by Baldwin in July 1909. Moody's notes on the back of this photograph read, "Construction number 33550. 35 inch drive wheels and 11 and a half X 14 inch cylinders."

On June 23, 1934, Moody returned to Franklin County to photograph the Sandy River. Ed West was the engineer that day, and Dana Aldrich was the fireman. Firemen and engineers make up the team that operates steam locomotives. The firemen tend to the boiler, making sure water is at the right level and shoveling coal and tending to the fire.

Here is another nice photograph of No. 18 at Strong on June 23, just off the turntable after a spin to line up the engine for the correct track.

The SR&RL main line is pictured at Avon on June 23, 1934. In this location, the rails were 52 to 58 pounds to the yard and were considered heavy rail for a two-foot-gauge railroad.

Moody is inspecting an SR&RL flatcar at Phillips. Most two-foot-gauge flatcars and gondolas were 33 feet long and 6 feet wide. (Photograph by Newell Martin.)

No. 18 is pictured on the Phillips turntable on June 23, 1934. Moody's notes on the back read, "Ed West in cab, Clarence Fairbanks at the end of the table, Dana Aldrich walking to the engine house and 'Happy' at the head of the table."

Newell Martin poses trackside east of Phillips at Avon. Martin lived in Massachusetts and was a frequent companion of Moody's when he traveled to photograph and study the Sandy River and Rangeley Lakes Railroad.

Turning around, Moody took another shot of the SR&RL main line in the opposite direction of where Newell Martin was standing in the previous image.

The SR&RL main line is seen just east of Howland's Crossing. Note the well-maintained track with good ballast and no weeds, even in the depths of the Great Depression.

The next trip to visit the SR&RL was on July 18, 1934, when Moody photographed a mixed train headed by No. 9. A mixed train is a passenger car combined with freight cars. It had paused in front of the Strong depot in this photograph.

The same mixed train is shown again pulled by 2-4-4 No. 9. It has backed into the Kingfield yard in front of the "new" depot, built in 1929 after a fire had destroyed the old covered station.

This image, taken at Phillips on July 18, 1934, shows No. 17 steamed up and still in winter attire. No. 17 had been rebuilt with a larger boiler by SR&RL's owner, Maine Central Railroad, in the winter of 1914 and 1915, arriving back in mid-February 1915.

Here is an interesting view from the front seat of REO railbus No. 5 on September 15, 1934. The location is just north of Farmington, near Fairbanks, and the railbus is heading north.

REO railbus No. 5 is at the Strong depot on an earlier trip to Farmington. Newell Martin was with Moody on this trip.

The other SR&RL REO railbus, No. 4, is making a connection with REO railbus No. 5 at Strong, just down from Kingfield. REO railbus No. 4 survives today at the Maine Narrow Gauge Railroad and Museum at Portland.

During this mid-September trip, Moody and Martin received news that the line and branches were to be removed and scrapped. They drove up to Rangeley to record this photograph of the depot there. The lines north of Phillips to Rangeley along with the branch lines to Barnjum, Madrid, and north of Eustis Junction had been dormant since the fall of 1931.

Walking down from the Rangeley depot on September 16, Moody took a good shot of the yard. The dismantling began just a few days later.

Eustis Junction is shown in this view looking west on September 16, 1934. The main line to Rangeley from Phillips is on the left, and the Eustis branch is to the right as it heads north. All were dismantled in the fall of 1934 and spring of 1935.

The Eustis branch is shown about a quarter mile north of Eustis Junction on September 16, 1934. Dismantling of the Eustis branch was finished in the spring of 1935.

Three

THE WW&F RAILWAY
OPERATIONS DERAIL

Linwood Moody visited and photographed the last train of the WW&F on June 15, 1934. This shot shows that little had changed from the opposite bank of the Sheepscot River. However, closer inspection reveals the minor vandalism that is unfortunately inevitable due to human nature. The combination car had some broken windows, and cigarette butts littered the floor.

This famous view of No. 8 and its train was photographed on June 15, 1934. No. 8's whistle was gone by then; perhaps it has survived in someone's collection?

On a trip a few days later, Moody found WW&F boxcar No. 312 on a siding with fading paint. Note the far end of the boxcar where a faded circular emblem of the original Wiscasset & Quebec Railroad was once painted.

On June 25, 1934, Moody returned to Albion where he was once depot agent for a day. Being depot agent at Albion was a lonely job and mostly involved helping load the Wiscasset-bound mixed train in the wee hours of the morning. On his last birthday on July 17, 1982, Moody told the author that he later had mixed feelings about quitting. He could see the WW&F was on its last leg and that helped influence his decision to quit after owner Frank Winter had misrepresented the job description. Albion was 43.5 miles from Wiscasset.

The WW&F Railway's enclosed water tank is shown just south of Albion on June 25, 1934. It was also known as Crosby's tank.

This view shows the WW&F main line looking north just outside Palermo, Maine, on June 25, 1934. Later that year, the main line rails were removed to pay a debt Frank Winter, the owner of the WW&F Railway, had neglected to take care of.

The Palermo Station, pictured on June 25, 1934, was 32.9 miles from Wiscasset and 10.6 miles from Albion. This station was converted to a home and survives to this day with modifications that most notably include removal of much of the overhanging roof.

The WW&F main line entered Palermo from the south. The station is in the distance along with a potato warehouse to the left of the station.

The WW&F station at China, shown on June 25, 1934, was 38.0 miles from Wiscasset and 5.5 miles from Albion. This photograph presents a rather lonely scene, with a lone boxcar on the siding.

This photograph shows the Weeks Mills station and its freight shed, which stills stands today. This was also known as Weeks Mills Junction for a few years until the line to Winslow was abandoned early in 1912 to 1914. Weeks Mills is 28 miles from Wiscasset and 15.3 miles from Albion.

The WW&F Windsor station is pictured on November 7, 1934. This station, a mile from the village of Windsor, or Windsorville, is 24 miles from Wiscasset and 19.2 miles from Albion.

On November 7, 1934, Moody found WW&F boxcars No. 67, No. 70, and No. 69 at the China siding. They never moved again on WW&F rails, as they were scrapped in place sometime in the late 1930s.

The WW&F trestle was photographed from the Atlantic Highway Bridge on November 14, 1934. Pictured are two railroad stations in the distance—the Maine Central Railroad to the left and the tiny WW&F station to the right with WW&F shop building behind in the distance.

Here is a good close-up of the WW&F office and station at Wiscasset on November 14, 1934, with the Maine Central Railroad's Rockland branch in foreground. The diamond crossing had been removed the previous year after the WW&F ceased operations. The large WW&F shop building is in the distance at far right.

The WW&F yard is pictured on November 14, 1934. Note the gondolas loaded with coal, never to be used in WW&F locomotives, as the railway ceased operations before it could be utilized.

Pictured on November 14, 1934, is the state road crossing a mile above Wiscasset. The scene is recognizable today, with a power line above the WW&F right-of-way.

The Head Tide station is seen on November 14, 1934. It was 9.1 miles north of Wiscasset and 34.4 miles from Albion.

This famous scene shows the WW&F main line rails being removed by a team of horses and a single flatcar on November 14, 1934, at the Head Tide siding. Moody's notes state that 100 rails equaled 3,500 pounds, a flatcar was 1,000 pounds, and four men were 600 pounds, making this load 45,600 pounds, or 22.5 tons.

The WW&F Railway's last train is sitting on the Head Tide siding after being moved there one by one by the team of horses. Locomotive No. 8 was left on the bank of the Sheepscot River, where it ended up at the time of its derailment.

Pictured here on November 14, 1934, the WW&F gravel pit was one mile above the Head Tide station. This gravel pit was where the WW&F got much of its ballast for its track. It was rather poor quality, more sand than gravel by several accounts.

This enclosed water tank was about one mile above Head Tide, and Moody's notes on the back say the photograph was taken on November 14, 1934. A replica of this tank was built by the Wiscasset, Waterville & Farmington Railway Museum at Sheepscot Station and can be seen in use today.

This is another famous scene recorded by Moody on November 14, 1934, of the horse-drawn flatcar being loaded with main line rails about a mile above the Head Tide water tank.

The abandoned grade of the WW&F at milepost 12 is shown here on November 14, 1934. The rails had just been removed by the horse-drawn flatcar and a seven-man scrapping team.

On his November 14, 1934, exploration, Moody found that the passage of one year had brought significant vandalism to the derailed locomotive No. 8. It was mostly superficial at this time, with a whistle missing, windows broken, and the results of normal outdoor exposure.

The Whitefield depot is pictured on November 14, 1934. It was 13.3 miles from Wiscasset and 29.2 miles from Albion.

Here is the North Whitefield station on November 14, 1934. This station was later converted to a storage building, but the notes on the back of the photograph do not reveal the year that work was completed. The station was 17.4 miles from Wiscasset and 26.1 miles from Albion.

Four

WINTER ON THE
SANDY RIVER RAILROAD

Moody traveled to the SR&RL Railroad in January 1935. In this photograph, SR&RL No. 10 with flanger and combination car ready is about to leave Phillips for Farmington in the late morning of January 18, 1935.

In this fascinating scene, No. 10 nearly hides itself with escaping steam. A few moments later, the train left Phillips for Farmington.

Here, just east of Phillips, is the SR&RL right-of-way just after passage of the No. 10 and its short train. Newell Martin was with Moody on the epic railfan trip in the depths of winter. Martin was a good friend of Moody's.

Locomotive 0-4-4 No. 17 and its train from Kingfield arrived at Strong to connect with No. 10's train headed to Farmington in the early afternoon on January 18, 1934.

In this interesting scene, the combination cars are sitting by the Strong depot while the two locomotives switched freight cars and No. 17 turned on the turntable. The Forney-type locomotives were preferred power for winter service with cozier enclosed cabs, and often their front-mounted snowplows were left on year-round.

Engine No. 24 is in front of the Strong station with No. 17 on the turntable. The Model A Ford was Newell Martin and Linwood Moody's transportation on this wintry day, January 18, 1934.

Engine No. 24 and some flatcars are hauling snow from the Strong yards. It was hauled a short distance and shoveled off the nearby trestle.

Later in the afternoon of January 18, Linwood Moody and Newell Martin arrived at Farmington to watch No. 10 switch; they had prepaid for the return trip back to Phillips. Fireman E'en Campbell is checking No. 10's running gear.

The snow was very deep in the Farmington yards on January 18, 1935. Fireman E'en Campbell has returned to the cab with engineer Dana Aldrich.

Sandy River No. 10 and the early evening train back to Phillips pauses at the Strong depot. Moody's notes read, "Taken at dusk on time exposure with camera held in hands. Note the lighted head light!"

Moody snapped a delayed action photograph of No. 10 at the Phillips water plug just before it was put to bed in the Phillips roundhouse at the end of a great winter railfan day on January 18, 1934. Newell Martin was with Moody on this trip.

This winter scene shows the bridge abutments of the Franklin, Somerset & Kennebec Railroad (FS&K) that were never completed due to inadequate funding. The FS&K was a subsidiary of the WW&F, and it was to connect with the Sandy River at Farmington and bridge the Kennebec River at Winslow to form a two-foot rail line from Farmington to Wiscasset. Moody often drove by this site on his way to Franklin County and the SR&RL Railroad.

Snow was still on the ground on April 1, 1935, as Sandy River No. 10 is turned on the turntable at the Farmington yard. It was good timing on the part of Moody and Newell Martin to show up and chase the train back to Phillips.

Moments later, No. 10 is facing the right direction for the return trip north. There was not much escaping steam from No. 10 that day.

No. 10 has backed down to hook up with its lone passenger car. From left to right are Dana Aldrich, engineer; E'en Campbell, fireman; and Bob McMullen, conductor.

The next stop on this April 1, 1935, trip is Strong, where a boxcar is added to the little train. Note the position of the ball signal by the depot behind the train. A ball signal was an early way railroads controlled access to rail yards as well as other railroads crossing each other. It was low tech, with no need for electricity.

No. 10 spots the boxcar in the yard just east and pulls the combine up to the station. No. 24's tender is outside as No. 24 is being repaired in the shop. Spotting a car means switching it to a certain location.

The No. 10 takes a spin on the Phillips turntable. Poor, out-of-service No. 22 is at left, having been there since its boiler flues had expired after 1926.

No. 10 comes off the turntable and is backing to the combination car it left in front of the depot on April 1, 1935.

On this trip, Newell Martin snapped this photograph of SR&RL railbus No. 4. In 1934, this railbus was re-engined with a six-cylinder Chevrolet motor. It kept its REO radiator and hood. Behind that was parked railcar No. 3 that had been re-engined with a Model A Ford engine and radiator. It was used to scrap the lines north of Phillips in 1934 and 1935.

Earlier in the day on the April 1 trip, Moody was left at Strong to ride the mixed train to Kingfield. It was pulled by 2-6-2 No. 18.

Combination car No. 14 is on the train back to Kingfield. The flat roof was a repair job done after the fire that destroyed the old Kingfield covered station. Combination car No. 14 had been found inside. The car was rescued, but the station was lost to the flames. Sadly, the "new" Kingfield depot, which was built in 1929, was recently lost in the 2010s due to a controlled burn.

The No. 18 that pulled the mixed train back to Kingfield needed coal, and the train crew was hand shoveling coal into the tender. The coal to power the SR&RL trains was stored in gondola cars at the rail yards at Phillips, Strong, Farmington, Kingfield, and other junction points wherever needed.

This photograph was taken while riding the Sandy River mixed train to Kingfield, near the summit at Salem station. Note the well-kept right-of-way. There were no saplings brushing the sides of the cars.

This photograph was taken from the other side of the combination car, near the summit. The grade was steep here, and the "stack music"—the loud noise coming from a hard-working steam locomotive—was great as it worked hard going up the grade.

No. 18 had arrived in Kingfield, turned on the turntable, and then backed down to couple up to its short train in front of the "new" station built in 1929. There is plenty of snow on the ground on April 1.

Here is No. 18 switching cars from the longer train it had brought in from Strong. Mount Abram is in the background. Newell Martin drove from Phillips up to Kingfield to pick up Moody, and the two stayed the night at the famous Herbert Hotel in Kingfield.

In this late-day shot, No. 18 is shown switching pulp wood cars to the mills at Kingfield. This concluded the April 1, 1935, trip to photograph the Sandy River. Time was running out for the SR&RL, as it would close down operations for good on July 2, 1935.

Five

Riding the Sandy River Mixed Train to Carrabasset

The next trip Moody made was to witness the last of the SR&RL operations on May 22, 1935. This series of photographs begins at Strong. Here, No. 24 is switching at Strong.

No. 24 goes for a spin on the turntable. The Strong depot is in the background to the left.

No. 24 is being turned by the train crew. The tall smokestack in the background at left is Forester's Toothpick Mill, a shipper on the SR&RL.

The mixed train departed Strong and is near North Freeman. Moody took this photograph from the back platform of combine No. 14. It survived and went to the Edaville Railroad. Today, it can be seen at the Maine Narrow Gauge Railroad and Museum at Portland.

The train has arrived at Kingfield. At left is the cute three-stall enginehouse that survived into the 1970s. It was sadly torn down to provide space for a car dealership parking lot.

The "new" depot in Kingfield is shown being built in 1929. It survived into the 2000s but was burned for practice by the local fire department. Only the shop building to the north survives.

This view shows the SR&RL trackage looking north on May 22, 1935, just south of Carrabasset.

This interesting view was taken from inside the cab of No. 24 at Carrabasset, looking south near the depot.

A very nice view from the tender of No. 24 is seen while paused by the Carrabasset depot. Ed West was engineer on this day.

In this classic view, No. 24 and its train sit beside the Carrabasset depot about ready to depart for Kingfield. Note Mount Bigelow in the background.

The last photograph of this series was taken on May 22, 1935, and shows the north end of the Carrabasset yard. The line continued on to Bigelow before 1927. A little bit of line remained to continue to Huston Brook to the end of operations a mile or so to the north.

The next series of photographs was taken from June 24 to June 27, 1935. This shot is of No. 18 pulling a train between Strong and Farmington on June 25.

No. 18 is seen with a mixed train at Strong on June 25 getting ready to depart Strong for Carrabasset with two extra coaches for 41 Civilian Conservation Corps (CCC) men. The CCC men were destined for Flagstaff, Maine, just north of Carrabasset. They went by open truck to their destination. The CCC built public works projects during the Depression days of the 1930s. It is not known what projects these men were working on.

SR&RL engine No. 18 pauses at Salem with the "CCC Special and Mt. Abram in the back ground," as Moody's notes state. The image was taken in the rain with a longer exposure.

The CCC Special mixed train arrives at Kingfield, and the sun has come out, an improvement over the rainy scene at Salem.

No. 18 and the CCC Special are about to depart Kingfield. The CCC boys were traveling to Flagstaff, but Moody's notes do not say what project they were traveling to work on.

The CCC Special mixed train arrives at Carrabasset on June 25, 1935. The CCC boys traveled by truck to get to their destination of Flagstaff. They traveled in style just in the nick of time, as the Sandy River shut down for good just a few days later.

The SR&RL mixed train leaves Phillips with a train of flatcars loaded with rail from the lines being scrapped north of Phillips. The date is June 26, 1935.

Six

The Last Operations of the SR&RL

This good photograph of the Reeds station was taken on June 26, 1935. Note the little Model A railcar in the distance pulling a load of rail from the line north.

This is another very nice photograph of the Reeds station. The Model A railcar is just out of sight to the left.

Pictured is the dismantling of the former Phillips & Rangeley Railroad near the bottom of Sluice Hill on June 26, 1935. All of this 35-pound rail was removed by hand.

This photograph is looking down grade on Sluice Hill not too far from Perham Junction where Moody's last birthday party was held many years later on July 17, 1982.

The SR&RL main line was near Cascade Brook on Sluice Hill. These rails were removed the very next day, June 27, 1935.

This is a view of the back side of Sluice Hill on June 26, 1935. All this rail was removed by hand by men working out of the Model A Ford railcar with its four-wheel bunk car and was taken away the next day on June 27, 1935.

The SR&RL Redington station is shown on June 26, 1935. The rail had been removed just two days before. The outhouse to the left of the station looks to be in poor condition, and another outhouse is attached to the station itself. Redington was once a busy place indeed.

This view of Redington is looking east on the same day as the previous photograph. The enginehouse once sat in the left foreground. There was also a small turntable for snowplows and track autos, like the Model A Ford railcar that was used to remove the rails.

In this photograph looking west at Redington, the rails were just removed two days ago. The trees are growing back rapidly, as train service had ceased on the lines west of Phillips in the fall of 1931.

This view of the SR&RL grade is looking east from Redington, down grade toward Sluice Hill, on June 26, 1935.

The next day, June 27, 1935, No. 24 leaves Phillips loaded with 35-pound rail that was recently removed. Fireman Ed West is visible in the engine cab.

Here is an interesting view of rail being loaded on a flatcar with the help of a 1928 Model A Ford roadster. The cable was tied to the front axle of the Ford, and it pulled the rails onto the flatcar.

Freshly loaded flatcar No. 410 is pictured. The removal of the lines north of Phillips kept the trains busy in the final days of common carrier operations. The trains kept busy after the shutdown too, but only with loads of scrap.

This interesting photograph shows the Sandy River depot at Phillips. Note the hardworking 1928 Model A Ford roadster taking a break from loading rail onto the flatcars.

Engine No. 24 brought empty boxcars to Phillips on July 1, 1935, as the SR&RL closed down operations. These trains ran as extras. Note the white card hanging from the headlight, indicating the train was an extra. An extra train is any that is not regularly scheduled.

The last common carrier train left Phillips on July 2, 1935. After that date, all trains were scrapping trains. On this last day, No. 24 and combine No. 14 run as an extra.

This is the SR&RL yard at Strong as it appeared on July 2, 1935. This photograph was taken from the back platform of combined No. 14.

Pictured is the last train at Strong on July 2, 1935. This view looking north shows Starbird's Mill as well.

To get this photograph, Moody was riding No. 24 sitting in the fireman's seat looking south near Starbird's Mill, near Strong.

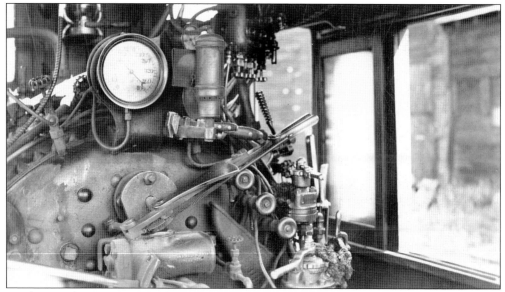

Sandy River locomotive No. 24's cab interior is shown in Farmington on July 2, 1935. This last train was a cleanup train, which simply means that it picked up all freight cars and brought them back to Phillips because the railroad was being closed down for good.

Here is another view of the interior of No. 24, looking from the tender. The last train went all over the operating sections of the SR&RL collecting rolling stock to take back to Phillips.

SR&RL No. 24 is pictured at Farmington after a spin on the turntable to face north where it will shortly couple up to its train. The crew on this day, July 2, 1935, is engineer Ed West in the cab, brakeman Norm Dustin, conductor Clarence Fairbanks, and a Mr. Thomas, the Maine Central Railroad's yardman.

This classic photograph is of No. 24 on the turntable with engineer Ed West in the cab. The photograph was taken at midday in the bright July sun.

No. 24 is about to depart the turntable area at Farmington and couple up to the cleanup train. It is bound for Phillips for the last time, except for scrap train runs.

Just north of Farmington, the cleanup train heads for Phillips. This very long train consists of empty boxcars and pulpwood cars being taken to Phillips.

The last long train whistles for the road crossing on the north edge of Farmington. The Russell Box factory is on the right.

The last train crosses the highway. The victorious trucks are stopped for the train, but they had the last laugh, as they now had all freight business north of Farmington.

Moody scrambled up onto the roof of combine car No. 14 for a better shot. The location is just north of Farmington on July 2, 1935.

The last train clips along between Farmington and Strong. Moody is still perched atop combine car No. 14.

The last train speeds along near Avon east of its final destination, Phillips. Moody is still atop the combine.

The crew stopped the train near an open field in Avon for a couple of final photographs. Moody had climbed down off the combine and hoofed it to the front of the train for this photograph. He then jumped the fence into the field at right.

This classic photograph shows No. 24 and its train next to a field in Avon on July 2, 1935. The author had three hand-painted, colorized photographs of this image made over 40 years ago. The best two went to Moody and Robert C. Jones (who used it in the second volume of his book *Two Feet Between the Rails*).

Engineer Ed West sparked the engine just after pulling the last train into Phillips on that sad July 2, 1935. He quickly walked into the roundhouse and later came back to run No. 24 inside.

Here is a very sharp picture taken by Moody of all the quiet locomotives sitting in the 10-stall roundhouse on that day of the last train run. From front to back are engine Nos. 21, 10, 16, 23, and forlorn engine No. 19 in the last stall. No. 19 had been out of service since 1928 due to boiler tubes having expired and no need for its use.

The light was good for a photograph due to the many windows on the south side of the roundhouse so Moody got a final shot of No. 19's cab interior. Poor No. 19 was trapped by No. 22 parked in front of its stall door.

No. 22 sits rusting outside of No. 19's stall, blocking the door. It was out of service as long as No. 19.

Moody returned on July 9 to find the new owners of the SR&RL were continuing the dismantling. The dismantling crew got to work on No. 22 first, and this photograph shows they were not wasting time. The line north of Phillips was not completely removed yet either.

Earlier in 1935, Moody had photographed the rapidly fading remains of the Wiscasset, Waterville & Farmington Railway. On March 3, he found boxcar No. 504 at North Whitefield sitting on a siding.

Also on March 3, Moody trudged through deep snow to visit and photograph the forlorn No. 8. Many parts were missing by then.

WW&F No. 8 is seen from a different angle on the same day. The deep snow did not deter Moody from making this visit.

Moody also returned to the yards of the WW&F at Wiscasset on March 3, 1935. The WW&F was deep in snow in quiet slumber.

Here is a view of the WW&F yard from atop the unused hopper coal car. The large shop building overshadows the rolling stock sitting idle on the yard tracks.

Jumping down from his coal-filled vantage point, Moody snapped this photograph of the WW&F's snowplow and flanger. They were built by the Portland Company.

Moody was able to gain access to the shop building and found WW&F Forney No. 3 slumbering. It was well worn but serviceable except for its boiler tubes, which had expired in 1932, inspiring owner Frank Winter to purchase the entire Kennebec Central Railroad for its two engines, which became WW&F Nos. 8 and 9.

Next to No. 3, WW&F No. 9 awaits rescue in 1937 by William Moneypenny. This lucky engine returned to Maine and is now restored to operation at the Wiscasset, Waterville & Farmington Railway Museum, just north of Wiscasset at Sheepscot Station in Alna, Maine. Here, dedicated members have restored 3.5 miles of track, and it is the best way to experience a Maine two footer today. If Moody were alive today, he would be very pleased at this wonderful organization. It certainly has been a dream come true for the author.

Seven

THE END OF A RAILROAD

Moody returned to the SR&RL the following year, 1936, to record the scrapping operations. He found Orris Vose's Model T railcar in Kingfield on June 19, 1936.

In this scene, the SR&RL is entering Kingfield from the south on June 19, 1936. The main line switch to Carrabasset is in the foreground by the water plug.

The Sandy River main line at South Strong is shown here on July 13, 1936. Weeds are taking over the soon to be scrapped rails.

The scrap train was hauled by No. 18 on July 13, 1936. The location is Strong Mountain on the main line to Farmington.

This is another view of SR&RL No. 18 on Strong Mountain. The date is July 13, 1936. It is patiently waiting while the scrapping crew does its work.

No. 18 is back in front of the Phillips roundhouse at 6:00 a.m. on July 14, 1936. The Salzberg's workday of scrapping began early.

The forlorn Strong depot awaits its end. It was torn down for its lumber just a couple short years after the SR&RL closed for good. The date is July 14, 1936.

This is Howland's gravel pit on August 14, 1936, about three miles east of Phillips in Avon. The remains of nearly 300 freight cars were burned here during the fall of 1935 and spring of 1936. As shown here, the scrap remains had yet to be hauled to Farmington.

The SR&RL main line between Strong and Avon at Cook's grade is pictured on August 14, 1936. Time is running out for the remaining line.

Just up the track from the previous view is a temporary repair to a washout. A spring storm in March 1936 created several washouts, causing the track bed to dissolve and leaving the rails and ties dangling in midair on the SR&RL main line. They were repaired in this manner so as to get the scrap trains to Farmington.

This photograph of the SR&RL roundhouse at Phillips was taken on August 14, 1936, just before the remaining engines were taken out to be scrapped.

SR&RL No. 17 is being hauled out to be scrapped. It was soon joined by Nos. 10, 23, and 9.

No. 17 is being turned on the turntable for the last time. Its headlight survives today at Phillips at the Sandy River Railroad Park where numerous examples of SR&RL rolling stock have been preserved. About a half mile of track has been restored to operation in the summer. It is well worth visiting.

No. 17 and its former crew pose for a photograph on August 14, 1936. From left to right are conductor Bob McMullen, engineer Fred Leavett, and brakeman Clarence Fairbanks.

A nice front view of No. 17 and its crew are shown on the same day as the previous photograph. From left to right are conductor Bob McMullen, engineer Fred Leavett, and brakeman Clarence Fairbanks.

SR&RL engine Nos. 17 and 9 are pictured after being hauled out of the roundhouse on August 14, 1936. No. 9 was hauled to Farmington as a backup engine but was never steamed again. No. 17 was scrapped shortly after.

Engine No. 23 is being hauled out of the roundhouse on August 14, 1936. That night, the roundhouse was empty of locomotives for the first time since it was built. This was the first time that No. 23 had been moved out since July 27, 1933.

This is the interior of the cab of engine No. 23. It was soon moved to Strong for temporary storage.

Engine No. 18 is ready to haul the big No. 23 to Strong. It turned out to be a temporary reprieve as it was later hauled back to Phillips and scrapped.

Here, No. 23 is arriving in Strong on August 14, 1936. It was parked next to the coal shed that was being torn down for its lumber.

No. 23 is being pulled by No. 18. Newell Martin and others, including Moody, rode in the cab of No. 23 over to Strong. In a letter to the author many years later, Moody stated he had reversed the No. 23's Johnson bar so the boiler pressure soon built up to 100 pounds, and for a short time, he admitted, he had the fiendish desire to blow the whistle. But he did not want to annoy Dana Aldrich, who allowed these railfans the fun of riding in the cab of No. 23.

No. 23 is waiting in Strong. Dr. Charles W. Bell of Strong had supposedly been interested in saving No. 23 and No. 10, but in the end, he chose not to. At least he saved parlor car No. 9, though, which survives to this day at Alna, stored for the Maine Narrow Gauge Museum inside its large car shed.

No. 10 is being hauled out of the roundhouse to be taken over to Strong that same day. Sadly, its whistle had already been removed. Its boiler was later found by Moody in the late 1950s in Portland. It disappeared after that encounter.

Here is a nice photograph of No. 10 being pulled to Strong by No. 18 at Hines Crossing, which was just to the left out of the photograph.

This is another nice shot of No. 10 on its way to Strong with its cab full of rail enthusiasts. Note the ball signal from the Strong yard sitting on No. 18's pilot.

Pictured is a more somber photograph of No. 18 hauling the last of the rails of the Kingfield branch to Farmington on this late August day in 1936.

In this September 9, 1936, photograph, taken by Kenneth Freeman of Trenton, New Jersey, SR&RL No. 18 and its scrap train are taking up the main line. The location was near Jack's Shanty. Moody surmised that this may be the last action shot of the Sandy River. The dismantling of the track was completed on September 15, 1936, at Farmington.

Here is an early morning view from the engineer's seat on July 13, 1936, on Strong Mountain, just two miles south of Strong.

Taken at the same time and location as the previous photograph, the wrecking crew seems to be taking a break in its somber task.

SR&RL No. 18 and No. 9 sit forlornly at the Farmington yard, remnants at the end of scrapping operations. No. 18 was still in steam at this time. The big REO railbus No. 5 is in front of the engines.

SR&RL   FARMINGTON SEPT. 13, 1936

"The End of a Railroad —"

THE LAST PICTURE EVER TAKEN AS A PART OF THIS
COLLECTION — (EXCEPT THOSE TAKEN BY OTHER PEOPLE)

SCENE SHOWS #18 ENGINE, UNDER STEAM, #9 ENGINE DEAD,
#5 REO RAILCAR. BEHIND REO IS THE TANK FROM #10
ENGINE.

The back of the previous photograph includes this example of Moody's handwriting. It shows in fact that it was "The End of a Railroad."

Eight

ODDS AND ENDS AND A VISIT TO THE MONSON RAILROAD

Moody visited the WW&F again in June 1936 and photographed the WW&F wharves. The wharves burned partially, and for some reason, Frank Winter rebuilt parts of the wharf with a plan that never materialized.

Also in June 1936, Moody snapped this photograph of the WW&F main line to the wharves that Frank Winter had rebuilt. Winter also wasted more of his money buying the two famous schooners at left. They lasted a long time, becoming at least a tourist attraction for the town of Wiscasset.

The WW&F Coopers Mills station is shown as it appeared on June 16, 1936. At this time, it had not been vandalized or broken into. Sadly, it burned to the ground a short time later. Coopers Mills was 20.4 miles from Wiscasset and 23.1 miles from Albion.

Moody made a trip to the Monson Railroad on November 10, 1938. His timing was good as Monson Railroad No. 4 was active that day.

Neglected Monson Railroad boxcar No. 2 was parked by the station and general offices on November 10. The depot still survives to this day.

Here is a view of a Monson Railroad siding on November 10, 1938, looking south toward Monson Junction.

Another shot of the Monson Railroad main line between Monson and Monson Junction shows that the track was still in reasonably good shape in 1939.

Monson Railroad No. 4 is both pushing and pulling its train to Monson Junction as was the usual, unconventional practice of operations of the Monson Railroad.

The Monson Railroad transfer yard at Monson Junction is shown here. The Bangor & Aroostook (B&A) Railroad was the wide-gauge connection. This photograph shows the difference between the two-footer rolling stock and its standard- or wide-gauge counterpart.

No. 4 is switching around the Monson Junction yard. Note the larger boxcar of the B&A, which dwarfs the No. 4.

Monson No. 4 is posed for Moody at Monson Junction. Posing with No. 4 is Sid Teweksbury. Moody's notes on the back of this photograph do not say if Teweksbury was a Monson Railroad employee or a friend of Moody's along for this trip.

Men hand shovel coal into Monson Railroad No. 4 on November 10, 1938—the same manner used for fueling *all* of the Maine two footers.

Here is the only photograph of the Bridgton & Harrison (B&H) Railroad in Moody's box of photographs that is the basis of this book. It shows B&H No. 8 at Bridgton Junction and has no dates or notes on the back. Moody may have had a box of B&H Railroad and Edaville Railroad photographs, but if he did, they may have been on loan at the time of his passing or otherwise lost to history. Most of his photographs of these two footers survive as negatives at the DeGolyer Foundation, fortunately.

Moody had some images by other photographers in his collection. This one is of Sandy River Railroad No. 1 after it received an overhaul.

SR&RL No. 19, which was formerly Sandy River Railroad's No. 8, is shown not long after it was renumbered. It is a shame that some photographs of it in its final years have not come to light. This was one of the SR&RL's most handsome engines.

This photograph is of Mount Gretna Narrow Gauge in southeastern Pennsylvania. This handsome little locomotive was built by Baldwin Locomotive Works of Philadelphia. It was abandoned in 1918.

This often reproduced photograph is of SR&RL Forney locomotive No. 6 and was sold by the SR&RL to the Kennebec Central Railroad in 1926. Frank Winter brought it to his WW&F in 1933. This lucky engine is in operation today at the Wiscasset, Waterville & Farmington Railway Museum.

This photograph of Linwood Moody was taken by the author on the occasion of Moody's 77th and last birthday on July 17, 1982. Moody is posing by the headstone of SR&RL engineer Dana Aldrich in the cemetery behind the site of the SR&RL 10-stall roundhouse in Phillips. There was still a pipe in his mouth and a watch fob in his pocket, and he wore a tie. In his front pocket is a package of Connecticut Cigars that was purchased on the way to Maine as a birthday gift.

Here is a photograph of Moody's friend Newell Martin, who joined Moody recording the SR&RL in film and photograph. Martin passed away in 1938, far too soon. Shortly before his death, Martin was able to travel west to Colorado to photograph a three-foot gauge. He rode the last Colorado & Southern train to Leadville, Colorado, in 1937 and rode the Denver & Rio Grande Western's "Shawano" to Gunnison, Colorado. He packed a lot into his short life.

This map from a 1908 official guide of the railways shows all the Maine two-foot railroads at that time.

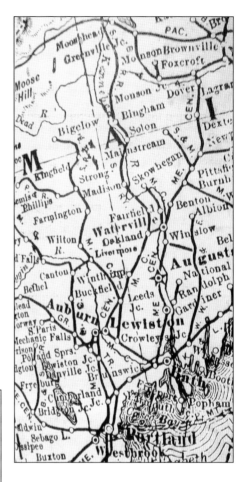

Phillips Me, Aug 30/33

Mr Linwood Moody

Union Me,

Dear Sir;

Your letter rec also the Pictures

and I thank you many times for them,

Weight of Eng 23 is 65 tons,

Iam unable to find the weights of the others

but will probably later,

Dia of the centers is 28" Tires are 35"

on the Eng you mention.

Hoping this is the information you desire

Iam ,

Truly Yours

L W Stinchfield

Master Mechanic

Here is a letter Linwood Moody received from SR&RL master mechanic Leland Stinchfield, thanking Moody for copies of the photographs of the engines that were pulled out of the roundhouse at Phillips by No. 16 on July 27, 1933. The photographs were taken by Moody at Stinchfield's request.

DISCOVER THOUSANDS OF LOCAL HISTORY BOOKS FEATURING MILLIONS OF VINTAGE IMAGES

Arcadia Publishing, the leading local history publisher in the United States, is committed to making history accessible and meaningful through publishing books that celebrate and preserve the heritage of America's people and places.

Find more books like this at
www.arcadiapublishing.com

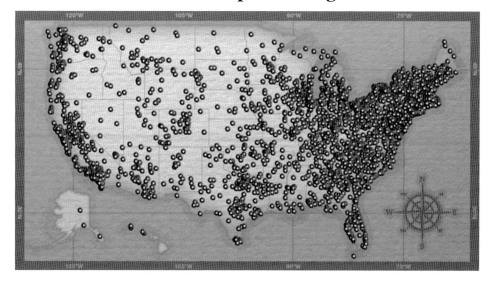

Search for your hometown history, your old stomping grounds, and even your favorite sports team.

Consistent with our mission to preserve history on a local level, this book was printed in South Carolina on American-made paper and manufactured entirely in the United States. Products carrying the accredited Forest Stewardship Council (FSC) label are printed on 100 percent FSC-certified paper.

MADE IN THE USA